RIVER FOREST PUBLIC LIBRARY
735 Lathrop Avenue
River Forest, Illinois 60305
708 / 366-5205

3/11

SUPER SANDCASTLE
Super Simple Cooking

Super Simple
Dinners

Easy No-Bake Recipes for Kids

Nancy Tuminelly

Consulting Editor, Diane Craig, M.A./Reading Specialist

ABDO
Publishing Company

Published by ABDO Publishing Company, 8000 West 78th Street, Edina, Minnesota 55439. Copyright © 2011 by Abdo Consulting Group, Inc. International copyrights reserved in all countries. No part of this book may be reproduced in any form without written permission from the publisher. Super SandCastle™ is a trademark and logo of ABDO Publishing Company.

Printed in the United States of America, North Mankato, Minnesota
052010
092010

♻ PRINTED ON RECYCLED PAPER

Editor: Katherine Hengel
Content Developer: Nancy Tuminelly
Cover and Interior Design and Production: Colleen Dolphin, Mighty Media
Photo Credits: Colleen Dolphin, iStockphoto (Tammy Bryngelson, Dawna Stafford), Shutterstock
Food Production: Colleen Dolphin, Kelly Dolphin

The following manufacturers/names appearing in this book are trademarks:
Target® Plastic Wrap, Pyrex® Measuring Cup

Library of Congress Cataloging-in-Publication Data

Tuminelly, Nancy, 1952-
  Super simple dinners : easy no-bake recipes for kids / Nancy Tuminelly.
    p. cm. -- (Super simple cooking)
  ISBN 978-1-61613-385-6
  1. Dinners and dining--Juvenile literature. 2. Quick and easy cookery--Juvenile literature. I. Title.
  TX737.T86 2011
  641.5'55--dc22
                        2009053112

Super SandCastle™ books are created by a team of professional educators, reading specialists, and content developers around five essential components—phonemic awareness, phonics, vocabulary, text comprehension, and fluency—to assist young readers as they develop reading skills and strategies and increase their general knowledge. All books are written, reviewed, and leveled for guided reading, early reading intervention, and Accelerated Reader® programs for use in shared, guided, and independent reading and writing activities to support a balanced approach to literacy instruction.

Note to Adult Helpers

Helping kids learn how to cook is fun! It is a great way for them to practice math and science. Cooking teaches kids about responsibility and boosts their confidence. Plus, they learn how to help out in the kitchen! The recipes in this book require very little adult assistance. But make sure there is always an adult around when kids are in the kitchen. Expect kids to make a mess, but also expect them to clean up after themselves. Most importantly, make the experience pleasurable by sharing and enjoying the food kids make.

Symbols

knife
Always ask an adult to help you cut with knives.

microwave
Be careful with hot food! Learn more on page 5.

nuts
Some people can get very sick if they eat nuts.

Contents

Let's Cook!

The recipes in this book are simple! You don't even need an oven or stove! Cooking teaches you about food, measuring, and following directions. It's fun to make good food! Enjoy your tasty creations with family and friends!

Bon appétit!

Cooking Basics

Before You Start...

- Get permission from an adult.
- Wash your hands. Wash all of your **produce** too.
- Read the recipe at least once.
- Set out all the ingredients, tools, and equipment you will need.
- Keep a towel close by for cleaning up spills.

When You're Done...

- Cover food with plastic wrap or **aluminum** foil. Use containers with tops when you can.
- Put all the ingredients and tools back where you found them.
- Wash all the dishes and **utensils**.
- Clean up your work space.

THINK SAFETY!

- Ask an adult to help you cut things. Use a cutting board.
- Clean up spills to prevent accidents.
- Keep tools and **utensils** away from the edge of the table or countertop.
- Keep pot holders or oven mitts close to the microwave.
- Use a sturdy stool if you cannot reach something.

Using the Microwave

- Use dishes that are microwave-safe.
- Never use **aluminum** foil or metal.
- Start with a short cook time. If you need to, add a little more.
- Use oven mitts when removing something.
- Stir liquids before and during heating.

Reduce, Reuse, Recycle!

When it comes to helping the earth, little things add up! Here are some ways to go green in the kitchen!

- Reuse plastic bags. If they aren't too dirty, you can use them again!

- Take a lunchbox. Then you won't use a paper bag.

- Store food in reusable containers instead of using plastic bags.

- Carry a reusable water bottle. Then you won't buy drinks all the time!

Measuring Tips

Wet Ingredients
Set a measuring cup on the countertop. Add the liquid until it reaches the amount you need. Check the measurement from eye level.

Dry Ingredients
Dip the measuring cup or spoon into the dry ingredient. Scoop out a little more than you need. Use the back of a dinner knife to scrape off the **excess**.

Moist Ingredients
Ingredients like brown sugar and dried fruit are a little different. They need to be packed down into the measuring cup. Keep packing until the ingredient reaches your measurement line.

Do You Know This = That?

There are different ways to measure the same amount.

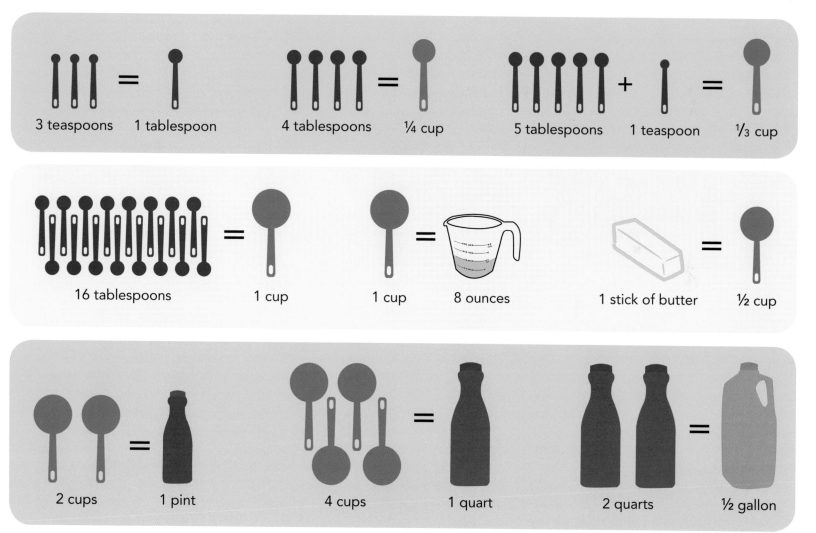

3 teaspoons = 1 tablespoon

4 tablespoons = ¼ cup

5 tablespoons + 1 teaspoon = ⅓ cup

16 tablespoons = 1 cup

1 cup = 8 ounces

1 stick of butter = ½ cup

2 cups = 1 pint

4 cups = 1 quart

2 quarts = ½ gallon

Cooking Terms

Chop
Cut into very small pieces with a knife.

Drain
Remove liquid using a strainer or colander.

Grate
Shred food into small pieces with a grater.

Mash
Crush food until soft with fork or masher.

Mix
Combine ingredients with a mixing spoon.

Peel
Remove fruit or vegetable skin. Use peeler if needed.

Pinch

Amount of an ingredient that can be held in fingers.

Slice

Cut into thin pieces with a knife.

Spread

Make a smooth layer with a spoon, knife, or spatula.

Toss

Turn ingredients over to cover with seasonings.

Using an Electric Blender

Put the base on the countertop. Make sure the jar is locked in place. Add the liquid ingredients, then the solids. Put the lid on tight. If you don't, you'll have a big mess!

Press the pulse button until all the ingredients are mixed. Do not over blend! Before you change settings, make sure the blade comes to a stop first.

When you're finished, pour the mixture into a glass or pitcher. Wipe off the base with a wet cloth. Wash the jar and lid with warm, soapy water. Be careful with the blade!

Tools

Here are some of the tools that you'll need to get started.

large container with lid

microwave-safe plate

can opener

measuring cup
(wet ingredients)

microwave-safe mixing & serving bowls

measuring cups
(dry ingredients)

blender

measuring spoons

cutting board

10

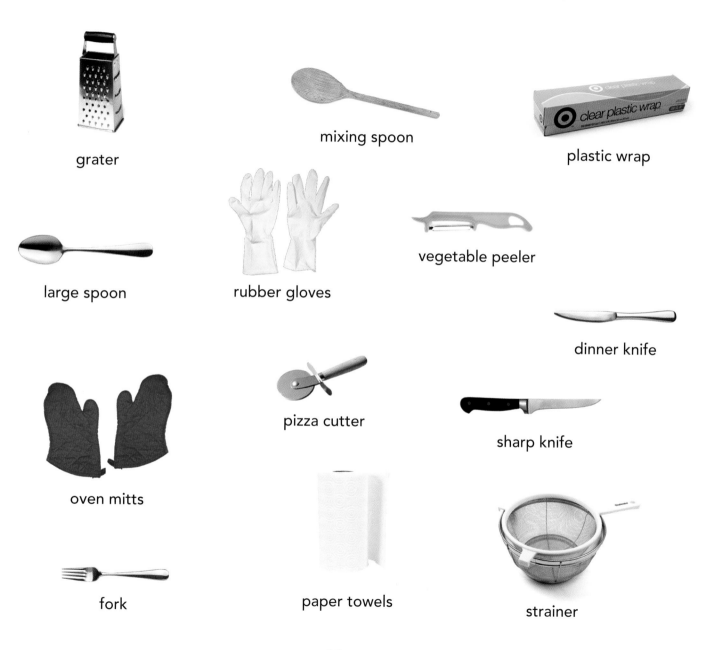

grater

mixing spoon

plastic wrap

large spoon

rubber gloves

vegetable peeler

dinner knife

oven mitts

pizza cutter

sharp knife

fork

paper towels

strainer

Ingredients

Fresh Produce

- tomatoes
- yellow onions
- celery
- cucumbers
- fresh dill
- fresh cilantro
- garlic cloves
- jalapeño peppers
- lettuce
- cherry tomatoes
- mixed salad greens
- red onions
- avocados
- zucchinis

- green tomatoes
- basil leaves
- shredded green cabbage
- Russet potatoes
- grated carrots
- broccoli florets
- green onions
- limes

Meat

- Italian salami

Canned Goods

- ☐ chickpeas
- ☐ water-packed tuna
- ☐ white beans
- ☐ kidney beans
- ☐ diced tomatoes
- ☐ diced green chilies
- ☐ pinto beans
- ☐ black beans

Dairy

- ☐ shredded mozzarella cheese
- ☐ feta cheese
- ☐ sour cream
- ☐ cheddar cheese
- ☐ butter
- ☐ cottage cheese
- ☐ plain yogurt
- ☐ grated parmesan cheese

Other

- ☐ olive oil
- ☐ white vinegar
- ☐ dry mustard
- ☐ pre-cooked pizza crusts
- ☐ black olives
- ☐ hummus
- ☐ Italian or Caesar salad dressing
- ☐ lime juice
- ☐ salsa
- ☐ taco shells
- ☐ sourdough buns
- ☐ chili powder
- ☐ cumin
- ☐ raw pine nuts
- ☐ baguettes
- ☐ lemon juice
- ☐ dill weed
- ☐ salt and pepper

Saucy Soup

Perfect for a cool summer supper!

Makes 4-6 servings

Ingredients

3 large ripe tomatoes, chopped

1 large yellow onion, chopped

2 celery ribs, chopped

1 cucumber, chopped

3 tablespoons olive oil

2 tablespoons fresh dill, chopped

1 tablespoon fresh cilantro, chopped

2 garlic cloves, chopped

1 teaspoon salt

1 fresh jalapeño pepper, seeded and chopped

1½ cups water

Tools

- rubber gloves
- sharp knife and cutting board
- measuring cups and spoons
- large mixing bowl
- mixing spoon
- blender
- large container with lid

1. Put on rubber gloves. Scoop out jalapeño seeds with spoon. Try not to touch your face or eyes. Chop jalapeño and other ingredients.

2. Put all ingredients in large bowl. Stir with mixing spoon.

3. Pour half mixture into blender. Blend on low for 20 minutes. Pour rest into blender. Continue to blend until smooth.

4. Put mixture in container. Cover and **chill** for at least 2 hours.

5. Spoon chilled soup into bowls. **Garnish** with chopped onion and sprig of cilantro. Serve with bread or cheese and crackers.

Chop-Chop Salad

A great antipasto for every salad lover!

Makes 6-8 servings

Ingredients

20-ounce bag lettuce

¼ pound Italian salami, chopped

1 cup shredded mozzarella cheese

1 cup canned chickpeas, drained and rinsed

5 tablespoons olive oil

2 tablespoons white vinegar

1 teaspoon dry mustard

½ cup parmesan cheese, grated

Tools

• sharp knife

• cutting board

• measuring cups and spoons

• can opener

• strainer

• large mixing bowl

• mixing spoon

• liquid measuring cup

1. To make salad, combine lettuce, salami, mozzarella cheese, and chickpeas in large bowl. **Chill** until ready to serve.

2. To make dressing, combine oil, vinegar, mustard, and parmesan cheese in liquid measuring cup. Stir well with mixing spoon.

3. Pour dressing over salad just before serving.

4. Toss lightly with two pieces of silverware. Serve on plates with bread.

Leftover salad can get really soggy. Keep leftover salad and dressing separate from each other. The lettuce will stay more crisp!

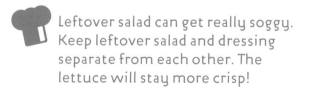

Opa Pizza

Pizza with Greek pizzazz!

Makes 8 servings

Ingredients

2 8-inch, pre-cooked
pizza crusts

½ cup hummus

½ cup cucumber, peeled
and sliced

½ cup tomato, chopped

½ cup feta cheese,
crumbled

Tools

- vegetable peeler
- dinner knife
- measuring cups
- sharp knife
- cutting board
- pizza cutter

1. Spread even amount of hummus on each pizza crust.

2. **Arrange** cucumber and tomato on top of hummus.

3. Top with feta cheese. Slice like pizza and serve. **Garnish** with salad!

 Try 4 **pitas** instead of two pizza crusts.

19

Vegetarian Taco Bar

A fun and healthy taco dinner!

Makes 4 servings

Ingredients

1 ripe avocado, skinned and pitted

15-ounce can chickpeas, rinsed and drained

3 tablespoons cilantro, chopped

4 teaspoons fresh lime juice

1 teaspoon garlic clove, chopped

salt and pepper

2 cups lettuce, shredded

1 cup salsa

½ cup sour cream

8 taco shells

Tools

• 4 medium bowls

• fork

• can opener

• strainer

• sharp knife and cutting board

• mixing spoon

• measuring cup

• 4 large spoons

Prepare avocado. See note below.
Place avocado in medium bowl.
Mash with fork.

 Add chickpeas, cilantro, lime juice,
and garlic.

 Salt and pepper to taste.
Set aside.

 To finish taco bar, put lettuce, salsa,
and sour cream in separate bowls.
Set next to bowl of avocado mixture.
Place large spoon in each bowl.

5 Heat taco shells in microwave for
15 seconds. Build your own tacos!

To prepare an avocado, slice it
lengthwise to the center seed.
Pull avocado apart. Lift out seed.
Use a spoon to scoop fruit from
the skin. It should come out easily.

Top Chef Salad

A 5-star salad fit for a meal!

Makes 4 servings

Ingredients

2 10-ounce bags of mixed salad greens

1 medium cucumber, peeled and sliced

8 cherry tomatoes, halved

12-ounce can water-packed tuna, drained

15-ounce can white beans, rinsed and drained

½ cup feta cheese, crumbled

¼ cup black olives, sliced

4 slices red onion, separated into rings

½ cup Italian or Caesar salad dressing

Tools

- vegetable peeler
- 4 dinner plates
- sharp knife
- cutting board
- can opener
- strainer
- measuring cups

Arrange lettuce evenly on each plate. Then arrange cucumber slices and tomato halves around edge of each plate.

 Add tuna to each plate. Place beans over tuna.

 Spread feta cheese and olives over tuna and beans.

4 Top with onion rings. Pour 2 tablespoons dressing over each salad.

 Try adding bell peppers, radishes, celery, and green beans. Serve with bread!

Chili Bean Bread Bowl

You can even eat the bowl!

Makes 4 servings

24

Ingredients

4 sourdough buns

16-ounce can black beans, drained and rinsed

16-ounce can kidney beans, drained and rinsed

14-ounce can diced tomatoes

4-ounce can diced green chilies

2 teaspoons lime juice

1 tablespoon chili powder

1 teaspoon cumin

¼ cup cheddar cheese, shredded

Tools

- sharp knife
- cutting board
- can opener
- strainer
- measuring cups and spoons
- mixing spoon
- large microwave-safe bowl
- plastic wrap
- oven mitts

1. Cut off top third of each bun. Pull out chunks of bread to make bowl. Leave ½-inch thick shell.

2. Mix beans, tomatoes, chilies, lime juice, chili powder, and cumin in large microwave-safe bowl.

3. Cover bowl with plastic wrap. Put in microwave on high for 2 minutes. Using oven mitts, remove and stir. Continue to microwave until chili mixture is very hot. Let stand for 1 to 2 minutes.

4. Spoon chili into bread bowls. **Garnish** each bowl with cheese.

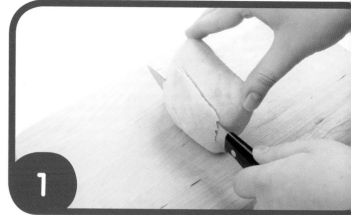

Green Pesto "Pasta"

Try these great veggie noodles!

Makes 4 servings

Ingredients

3 medium zucchini, peeled

1 medium green tomato, chopped

1 tablespoon olive oil

salt and pepper

2 cups fresh basil leaves

1 garlic clove, finely chopped

½ cup raw pine nuts

¼ cup plus 2 tablespoons olive oil

1 teaspoon salt

¼ teaspoon black pepper

Tools

• vegetable peeler
• sharp knife
• cutting board
• large bowl
• mixing spoon
• measuring spoons & cups
• blender
• plates

1. Cut zucchini into strips **lengthwise**. Throw out center with seeds. Slice strips into "noodles."

2. Put noodles in large bowl. Mix tomato and olive oil with noodles. Salt and pepper to taste. Set aside.

3. To make pesto, put all remaining ingredients in blender. Blend on **purée** setting until pretty smooth. Some pine nuts pieces are all right.

4. Gently mix pesto with noodle and tomato mixture until coated.

5. Spoon mixture onto plates. **Garnish** with any extra pine nuts and basil leaves.

 Serve with bread and green salad! Yum!

27

Sombrero Sandwich

Scrumptious supper surprise!

Makes 4 servings

Ingredients

15 ounces pinto beans, rinsed and drained

3 tablespoons salsa

1 tablespoon jalapeño pepper, chopped

½ teaspoon ground cumin

1 ripe avocado, skinned, pitted and chopped

2 tablespoons red onions, chopped

1 tablespoon lime juice

1 baguette, 16 to 20 inches long

1⅓ cups green cabbage, shredded

Tools

- can opener
- strainer
- measuring cups and spoons
- mixing bowls
- fork
- sharp knife
- cutting board

Mash beans, salsa, jalapeno, and cumin together in medium bowl with fork.

 Mash avocado, onion, and lime juice in small bowl with fork.

 Cut baguette into four equal pieces. Split each piece **lengthwise**. Pull out most of soft bread in center.

 Cover bottom of each baguette piece with cabbage. Put equal amount of avocado mixture and then bean mixture on the cabbage.

 Place top on each baguette piece and serve!

To prepare avocado, see page 21!

Tasty Taters & Toppings

A filling gourmet dinner delight!

Makes 4 servings

Ingredients

4 large Russet potatoes

4 tablespoons sour cream

4 tablespoons butter

1 cup cheddar cheese, shredded

Tools

- forks
- paper towels
- sharp knife
- cutting board
- measuring cups
- measuring spoons
- plates
- oven mitts
- grater

1 Wash potatoes and pierce each one four times with fork.

2 Wrap each potato in paper towel. Place them 1 inch apart in microwave. Microwave on high for 5 minutes. Turn potatoes over. Microwave for 5 more minutes.

3 Turn and microwave for 1 minute at a time until soft. Let potatoes sit for 2 minutes. Remove paper towel wraps.

4 Cut each potato in half **lengthwise**. Mash inside with fork.

5 Top each with 1 tablespoon butter and 2 tablespoons cheese.

6 Return to microwave. Cook on high until cheese melts. Put potato on plate and top with remaining cheese and sour cream. Or try them with Cheesy Dill Topping or Salsa Topping!

4

Cheesy Dill Topping

1 cup cottage cheese

½ cup plain yogurt

3 teaspoons lemon juice

6 green onions, chopped

1 teaspoon dill weed

Salsa Topping

¼ cup prepared salsa

¼ cup cheddar cheese, shredded

2 tablespoons sour cream

½ cup grated carrots

1 cup broccoli florets, microwave steamed

Glossary

aluminum – a light metal.

arrange – to place in a certain order or pattern.

chill – to put something in the refrigerator to make it cold or firm.

excess – more than the amount wanted or needed.

garnish – to decorate with small amounts of food.

lengthwise – in the direction of the longest side.

pita – a thin, flat disk of bread.

produce – things that are grown for eating, especially fruits and vegetables.

purée – to make very smooth and creamy using a blender.

utensil – a tool used to prepare or eat food.